SPACE SHUTTLE

Robin Kerrod

NASA
905
United States

SPACE SHUTTLE

Columbia
NASA
United States

CONTENTS

All photographs used in this book were kindly supplied by NASA.

This book was devised and produced by Multimedia Publications (UK) Ltd.

Editor Jeff Groman
Design Mick Hodson
Picture Research Jane Williams

ISBN 0 8317 7964 0

First published in the United States of America by Gallery Books, an imprint of W.H. Smith Publishers Inc., 112 Madison Avenue, New York NY 10016
Originated by D S Colour International Ltd, London
Printed by Verlag Buch und Welt, Austria

INTRODUCTION

On 12 April, 1981, an entirely different kind of space vehicle was put through its paces for the first time. The vehicle was an airplane-like craft called *Columbia,* which soared into orbit from the Kennedy Space Center in a spectacular fireworks display witnessed live by an audience of nearly a million people.

In November of the same year *Columbia* repeated the performance and made space history. It was the first time that any craft had returned to space. Ordinary launching rockets are expendable – they can be used only once. When their work is done, they either fall into the sea, burn up in the atmosphere, or remain in orbit as so much space junk.

Columbia, then, was unique. And as if to prove the point, it made another three trips into orbit in 1982. It is unique no longer because it has been joined by two sister craft, *Challenger* and *Discovery.* These three craft are the major hardware of NASA's space shuttle transportation system and will be joined soon by a fourth craft, *Atlantis.* These vehicles are the orbiters, which are part rocket ship, part glider. They take off vertically from a launch pad like a rocket, but land horizontally on a runway like an ordinary plane.

The space shuttle has become the major space launching system of the United States, carrying into orbit most domestic and many foreign satellites. Its main rival for satellite launchings in the Western world is the European launcher *Ariane,* which now has many successful flights to its credit.

But it is not only for satellite launchings that the shuttle has been designed. It also carries other important cargo into orbit, such as the European-built Spacelab. It has enabled an expanding corps of American and foreign astronauts, women as well as men, to experience the topsy-turvy world of space for the first time. Further, it has proved to be useful as a service station for retrieving and repairing ailing satellites in orbit.

The Beginnings

Although the shuttle transportation system has only just come to fruition, the concept of a re-usable spacecraft predates the Space Age. As early as 1950 the much respected British Interplanetary Society (founded 1933) was discussing a re-usable manned orbital rocket system. It featured a winged glider that was lofted into space atop a booster rocket. One of the founding fathers of modern rocketry, Wernher von Braun, developed a similar theme in articles he wrote for *Colliers* magazine a few years later.

However, in the headlong rush into space in the late 1950s, the re-usable concept was abandoned. Attention was focused on getting into space, whatever the cost. By the early 1960s the United States was racing for the Moon, and had landed astronauts there by the end of the decade. The euphoria attending this magnificent achievement was short-lived. Launching human beings and satellites into space in expendable craft was very expensive and wasteful. The need for a more economical system became pressing.

So in 1970 NASA set in motion design studies for a re-usable space transportation system that eventually resulted in the present space shuttle. Seven years later a prototype orbiter, *Enterprise,* was ready for its first flight tests in the atmosphere. But problems with the engines and heat-shield materials prevented the shuttle making its space debut until *Columbia* rose majestically into orbit on 12 April, 1981. Truly, a new era in space exploration dawned that day.

Viewed through the open doors of the Vehicle Assembly Building, the prototype orbiter *Enterprise* begins its slow journey to the launch pad in 1979 in a dummy run to verify operating procedures. But it will be another two years before the first working orbiter becomes operational.

USA

1 UP UP AND AWAY

The main operating base for the space shuttle is the Kennedy Space Center in Florida. Shuttle activity is centered on Complex 39, which was developed in the 1960s for the Apollo Moon-landing missions. For the shuttle era the facilities have been modified and updated. Dominating the Complex still is the huge Vehicle Assembly Building (VAB), built to house the 305-foot (111-meter) tall Apollo-Saturn Moon rocket and now altered for the assembly of the shuttle. From the VAB, a broad graveled crawlerway leads to the launch pad, some 3.5 miles (5.5 kilometers) away.

When the shuttle assembly leaves the VAB for the pad, the orbiter is sitting on its tail on the mobile launching platform. It is attached to an external tank, which will provide fuel for its engines. Strapped to the side of this tank are twin booster rockets. Carrying the mobile launch platform at a snail's pace is an eight-tracked crawler transporter, by far the world's biggest land vehicle, measuring 131 feet by 114 feet (40 meters by 35 meters).

On arrival at the pad the transporter drops its load and returns, fractionally faster, to its parking lot next to the VAB. Meanwhile on the pad the shuttle stack is being connected with the service tower, and the preliminary preparations for launching begin.

With only about three days left before lift-off, the final countdown begins. Technicians and ground controllers begin going methodically through an extensive check list of operations to verify that the many hundreds of shuttle systems are functioning properly.

Lift-off!

With just two hours to go before lift-off, the crew enter the cockpit. Then the pad is cleared of all personnel. Nine minutes to go, and the final automatic launch sequence begins. Seven seconds to go, and the orbiter's main engines start and throttle up to full power. Zero: the rocket boosters ignite, explosive connectors holding the shuttle down to the pad are severed, and we have lift-off.

The launch pad erupts into flame as the shuttle surges heavenwards. Seconds after clearing the tower the shuttle rolls over onto its back, accelerating all the while. In less than a minute it is traveling at more than Mach 1, the speed of sound, and is virtually out of sight from the ground. After two minutes it is traveling at more than Mach 4 and is nearly 28 miles (45 kilometers) high.

By now the fuel in the booster rockets is exhausted, and they are blasted free from the external tank. They arc up and over and then down towards the sea. At an altitude of about 3 miles (5 kilometers) their nose caps are jettisoned and parachutes are deployed which slow down their descent and lower them to a gentle splashdown. Waiting ships take them in tow and return them to the launch center.

Into Orbit

The shuttle, now consisting only of orbiter and external tank, meanwhile continues to gather speed and height as its main engines consume more than 60,000 gallons (270,000 liters) of fuel every minute.

At a height of about 75 miles (120 kilometers) the fuel in the external tank is nearly gone and the main engines cut off. A few seconds later the external tank separates and follows an arcing trajectory that will take it, or what is left of it, into the Indian Ocean.

After main engine cut-off, the orbiter coasts for a while before firing two smaller engines of the orbital maneuvering system. This boosts its speed to about 17,500 mph (28,000 kilometers an hour), and allows it to enter orbit. At this orbital

With a thundrous roar orbiter *Challenger* accelerates off the launch pad on the tenth shuttle mission in February 1984. Its five-man crew includes Bruce McCandless and Robert Stewart, who are destined to make the world's first untethered spacewalks using the manned maneuvering units. In orbit the crew will also deploy a number of satellites and oversee several experiments.

USA
United States
NASA
Challenger

velocity, it will continue circling round and round the Earth without the need for further engine boost. This happens in orbit because there is no air resistance to slow the orbiter down. Typically, the orbiter travels in an orbit about 150-200 miles (240-320 kilometers) high, and takes about one and a half hours to circle the Earth.

Fiery Re-entry

At the end of the shuttle mission the orbiter prepares to return to Earth. The return journey is considerably more hazardous than the take-off. When it drops from space, the orbiter has to change gradually from a rocket ship to an aircraft, which is a very tricky operation. And the descent is unpowered – there is no fuel for the orbiter's main engines. So once the orbiter is committed to land, it must land – there is no going round for a second try.

The first thing the orbiter must do to return to Earth is to brake. It must slow down to below orbital velocity so that the Earth's gravity can capture it. The orbiter brakes by first turning back to front so that it is traveling tail first. The orbital maneuvering system engines then fire again, slowing it down.

As it slowly loses height, the orbiter pitches over into a forward-pointing, nose-up attitude. At a height of about 400,000 feet (120,000 meters) it plunges into the outer fringes of the atmosphere: speed of travel, 25 times the speed of sound. Friction with the air molecules generates a tremendous amount of heat, which raises the temperature of the outer shell of the orbiter to as much as 1,500°C. The underside of the craft, coated with thick ceramic tiles takes the brunt of the re-entry heating and glows red-hot. The ceramic material is a superb insulator, however, and the orbiter's airframe and the crew inside remain cool.

Heading for Touchdown

For about a quarter of an hour during re-entry, communications between the orbiter and ground control are interrupted. Radio waves are unable to pass through the very hot, ionized air layer around the craft. When the orbiter comes out of the radio blackout, it is traveling like an aircraft and using its rudder and wing control surfaces to maneuver. The drag of the air has slowed it down to about five times the speed of sound. It loses more speed as it performs a series of slow rolls and then swoops down to the runway at an angle of 22° – seven times more steeply than an airliner.

At an altitude of only 1,700 feet (520 meters) the orbiter's nose begins coming up to flatten the glide slope. At about 90 feet (27 meters) the landing gear extends and touchdown takes place about 15 seconds later at about 200 mph (320 kilometers an hour). Air brakes on the rudder and wheel brakes slow the orbiter down in about 7,000 feet (2,000 meters). But there is plenty of runway left in case of emergencies. The early shuttle flights landed at the Edwards Air Force Base in California, but the regular landing site is at the Kennedy Space Center, close to the VAB. The first landing at Kennedy took place early in 1984 on the eleventh shuttle mission. There is another purpose-built shuttle landing runway at the Vandenberg Air Force Base in California, which has now become operational as a second shuttle launch site. It has slightly different launch facilities from Kennedy and is suited for launching spacecraft that need to be placed in orbit over the poles. It is also the prime launching site for military payloads.

Main picture: A surrealistic early morning scene at the Kennedy Space Center, captured in this dramatic aerial photograph. It shows the shuttle assembly making its slow journey through dense ground mist towards the launch pad.

Below left: A huge crawler transporter carries the shuttle assembly along the graveled crawlerway leading from the Vehicle Assembly Building (visible in the background). It is on its way to the launch pad 3.5 miles (5.5 kilometers) away. The journey will take between 5 and 6 hours. The shuttle assembly, comprising orbiter, solid rocket boosters and external tank, is mounted on a mobile launch platform which the crawler will place in position on the pad.

Below right: The shuttle stack is now in position on the launch pad at Complex 39A. With only a few days to go before launch, the countdown is about to begin. The pad will soon be crawling with technicians carrying out the thousands of pre-flight checks needed to ensure a trouble-free lift-off.

Left: The countdown clock stands at zero. Orbiter *Challenger's* main engines are reaching full power. Then the solid rocket boosters ignite and the shuttle lifts off the pad. Within seconds it has cleared the tower and is heading for orbit. The take-off is always spectacular to watch but never more so than at night, as here in August 1983.

Above: Surging upwards at ever-increasing speed, the shuttle becomes a tiny luminous spot atop a plume of steam and smoke. Soon the solid rocket boosters will be separating. This shot was taken by veteran astronaut John Young in a shuttle training aircraft.

Right: A spectacular view of the lift-off of orbiter *Columbia* a fraction of a second after the solid rocket boosters have ignited. It is recorded by a remote camera on the service gantry. No human photographers are allowed within 3.5 miles (5.5 kilometers) of the launch pad.

FACC
30

Left: Controllers discuss shuttle pre-launch operations in the Launch Control Room at the Kennedy Space Center. It is a glass-fronted building located at the base of the Vehicle Assembly Building, looking towards the launch pad. The controllers there coordinate all activities on the pad and in the shuttle until a few moments after lift-off.

Right: The jubilant scene in the Launch Control Room after the successful launch of the first shuttle on 12 April, 1981. Two days before, the first attempt at launching ended in failure and a million people in and around the Kennedy Space Center went home disappointed.

Below: When the shuttle has cleared the launch pad tower, responsibility for communications and flight control passes to the Johnson Manned Spaceflight Center at Houston in Texas. Here, the mission operations control room acts as the nerve center for each mission. Ground controllers, each with special responsibilities, sit at communications consoles with video screens, upon which they can display all relevant information.

Below: The shuttle's solid rocket boosters fire for approximately two minutes before their fuel is exhausted. Then they separate from the orbiter and its external fuel tank. As they plummet Earthwards, parachutes open above them and lower them to a gentle splashdown in the Atlantic Ocean. Within minutes recovery ships waiting in the splashdown area take them in tow.

Below: The external fuel tank supplies liquid hydrogen and liquid oxygen to the shuttle's main engines for about 8 minutes after launch. Then it runs dry, and separates from the orbiter. This on-board picture shows the tank moments after separation. It will now plunge back to Earth, burning and breaking up in the atmosphere before falling into the Indian Ocean.

NASA's booster recovery ship *Liberty* tows one of the two solid rocket boosters through Port Canaveral following recovery in the Atlantic. The booster will eventually be dismantled and then refurbished for use on a future shuttle flight.

Above: Up in orbit some 150 miles (240 kilometers) above the Earth, *Challenger* fires the orbital maneuvering system engines in its tail to change position. At the end of the mission the engines will fire again to slow down the orbiter so that it can drop from orbit and start its hour-long descent to Earth.

Below: Flanked by a T-38 chase plane, orbiter *Columbia* glides towards the runway at the Edwards Air Force Base in California on 14 April, 1981. The touchdown, seconds later, is historic, marking the end of the first successful shuttle mission.

Above: The returning orbiter makes a series of loops and turns after re-entering the atmosphere. In this way it loses speed more rapidly and lines itself up for landing on the runway. Only minutes ago the black insulating tiles on the underside were glowing red-hot.

Below: Orbiter *Challenger* glides to a perfect touchdown at night on 5 September, 1983. Six days earlier it had made the first night-time take-off. The night launch and landing prove the 24-hour operating capability of the shuttle system, which could be important for future missions to rescue astronauts stranded in orbit.

Left: Immediately after the orbiter lands, ground support trucks move in. They remove gases and excess fuel from the orbiter and perform other safety operations before the astronaut crew emerges.

Right: Smiling broadly, the six-man crew of the ninth shuttle flight exits from *Columbia* after a record 10-day mission in November 1983. The mission marks the first flight of the European space laboratory *Spacelab* and the first flight of a non-American astronaut. He is Ulf Merbold from West Germany (third from top).

Below: After each shuttle flight the crew undergo immediate debriefing by NASA personnel. Some time afterwards they meet the press at a post-flight press conference. Here, first American woman astronaut Dr Sally Ride answers a reporter's question, while Bob Crippen (left) and Fred Hauck look on.

2 Getting it Together

When NASA began design studies for a re-usable space transportation system in the early 1970s, it first considered a fully re-usable system. The crew and payload (cargo) would travel in a large winged, rocket-powered craft, which would be carried into orbit by a larger winged booster aircraft, also manned. This scheme, however, proved far too expensive. So it was decided to go for a smaller orbiting craft, with an external fuel tank, and to use unmanned rockets as boosters.

The present shuttle system emerged – winged orbiter, external fuel tank and twin boosters. Of this hardware, only the external tank is expendable. Orbiter and boosters are used time and time again. It is expected that the orbiters will have a long life span and be able to travel into space and back up to 100 times. Then they will undoubtedly be replaced by larger 'Supershuttles', capable of reaching higher orbits and carrying larger payloads.

The Boosters and External Tank

The most vital component of the shuttle hardware is the crew-carrying orbiter. This rides into space piggy-back on the much larger external tank, to which are attached the twin boosters. It sheds these appendages in turn as it rockets into orbit.

The external tank is designed to hold the fuel, or rather the propellants, for the orbiter's main engines. It has two tanks – one containing liquid hydrogen, the other liquid oxygen. These propellants are cryogenic – they are very cold indeed (–253°C and –183°C). The aluminum structure of the tank is protected from temperature extremes during lift-off and ascent by thick plastic foam, which gives the tank its distinctive orange-brown color.

The rocket boosters are by contrast made from welded steel segments for they must be tough enough to survive multiple impacts with the ocean. They contain solid propellant material in which the fuel is primarily aluminum powder. In the nose are housed the parachutes that slow their descent to the ocean after lift-off.

The Versatile Orbiter

The shuttle orbiter is the most advanced flying machine ever made and the only one designed for traveling in space as well as in the atmosphere. It looks very much like an airplane, having wings and a tail, which stabilize its flight through the air. And it maneuvers in the air by means of control surfaces on the wings (elevons) and tail (rudder). With a length of some 122 feet (37 meters) and a wing-span of 78 feet (24 meters) it is about the same size as a medium-range airliner like the DC-9.

However, unlike an airplane it has rocket engines rather than jet engines (which require air from the atmosphere) and can therefore function in space. It is also equipped with sets of rocket thrusters which enable it to maneuver in space where wings and tail, elevons and rudder are useless.

The crew occupy the forward fuselage of the orbiter, which is pressurized to normal sea-level pressure. This is split into an upper and mid-deck with storage lockers beneath. The upper level is the flight deck which has seating capacity for a crew of up to seven. The pilot and commander for the mission sit in front in the cockpit, which looks very similar to the cockpit of a conventional airliner. A major difference, however, is the presence of three video screens, which display data from the computer system that effectively controls all on-board operations.

The mid-deck of the orbiter is the main living area for the crew. This is where they eat, sleep and wash. In the mid-deck too is an airlock, which leads into the cargo bay of the orbiter. The cargo, or payload, bay is enormous, measuring some 60 feet (18 meters) long and 15 feet (4.5 meters) across. It can carry payloads weighing up to 30 tons. Unlike the forward

The prototype shuttle orbiter *Enterprise* glides in to land at Edwards Air Force Base in southern California in October 1977. It was carried aloft by a modified Boeing 747 and released at an altitude of about 20,000 feet (6,000 meters).

United States

fuselage, the payload bay is unpressurized. Astronauts have to wear spacesuits if they want to enter it.

Beneath the payload bay are a number of tanks of liquid hydrogen and liquid oxygen. These provide fuel for the system that produces electrical power on board. The system depends on fuel cells, ingenious chemical devices which generate electricity by combining hydrogen and oxygen to form water. By so doing they ensure a plentiful supply of water for drinking, cooking and washing.

The three main engines of the orbiter are clustered in the tail. They burn liquid oxygen and liquid hydrogen, which are both carried in the external tank. Also located in the tail are the two engines of the orbital maneuvering system (OMS), which fire to insert the orbiter into orbit at the beginning of a mission, and to slow it down so that it drops from orbit at the end of a mission. Sets of rocket thrusters, used for maneuvering in space, are grouped near each OMS assembly and also in the orbiter's nose.

The Flying 'Brickyard'

This nickname has been given to the shuttle orbiter, and it is quite an apt one. The underside of the orbiter is covered by thick chunks of ceramic material, made from silica. Elsewhere, thinner sections of ceramics are used, but thick or thin they are all generally known as tiles.

These tiles form the major part of the insulating outer surface, or heat shield of the orbiter. Over 34,000 of them were used on *Columbia,* the first orbiter. On parts of the surface subjected to the highest temperatures – the nose and leading edges of the wings – a special carbon refractory material is used. But in low-temperature areas, such as the upper fuselage, a flexible insulating felt is adequate.

The tiles are stuck one by one onto the aluminum airframe of the orbiter and have a remarkable insulating capacity that protects the orbiter from temperatures of up to 1,500°C. However, they are extremely brittle and could be cracked during a violent hailstorm. Initially there were also difficulties with bonding the tiles, and many fell off when the orbiters were flown in to the Kennedy Space Center after assembly. It was feared that the loss of tiles in a high-temperature area could lead to the airframe burning away locally and crippling a vital system or perhaps causing a lethal depressurization. In practise so far, the tiles have performed well and remained more or less intact. But they are thoroughly checked over after each mission and replaced if necessary.

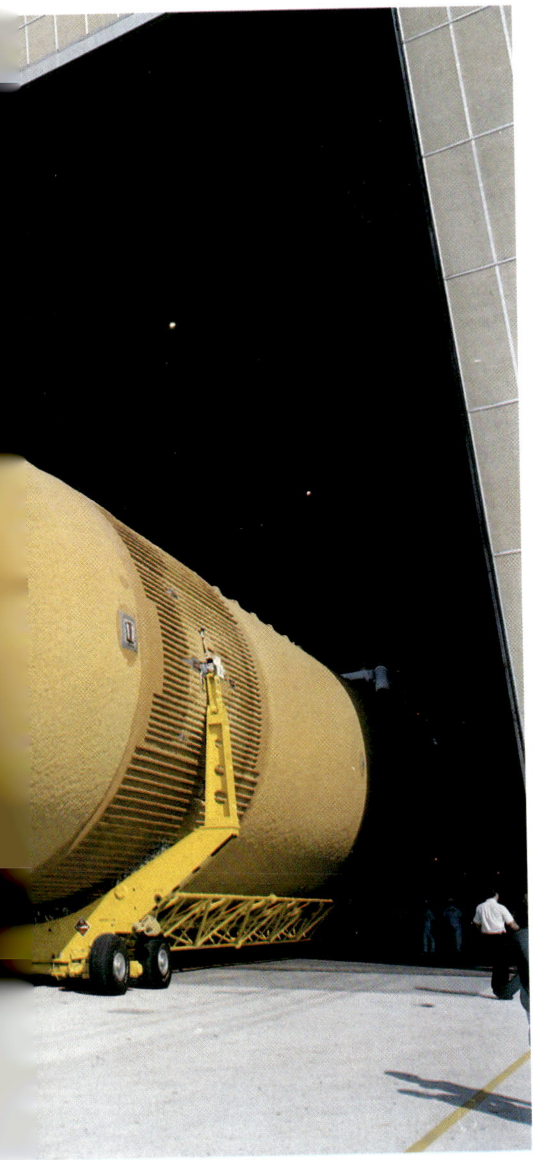

Top left: Steam, smoke and flames billow from the nozzle of a solid rocket booster, during a test firing at a site in Utah. During the two-minute firing the motor's thrust reaches a peak of some 3,000,000 pounds (1,360,000 kilograms). The shuttle uses two such boosters at lift-off, which separate and parachute back to Earth after about two minutes.

Above: Scale models of the shuttle solid rocket boosters are dropped during impact tests at Long Beach Naval Station in California. These tests are carried out to ensure that no damage is sustained by the real boosters when they parachute back to Earth after each shuttle launch.

Left: The huge external fuel tank of the shuttle making its way to the Vehicle Assembly Building (in the background). It has just been off-loaded from the barge that has carried it from the manufacturers in New Orleans. It measures 154 feet (47 meters) long and is over 27 feet (8 meters) in diameter.

Above: Inside the massive Vehicle Assembly Building the external fuel tank is being mated to the twin solid rocket boosters. When the tank is in position, the orbiter will be lowered onto it, and the assembly will be complete. The Vehicle Assembly Building was built in the 1960s to assemble the 365-feet (111-meter) high Apollo-Saturn Moon rocket and was modified for use with the space shuttle.

Left: A one-third scale model of the shuttle orbiter is installed in a wind tunnel at NASA's Ames Research Center in California. As with all aircraft, wind-tunnel tests of scale models are essential to check that the aerodynamic design is sound.

Below: Nearly complete, orbiter *Columbia* is seen in the production bay of its manufacturers, Rockwell International, at Downey in California. Details of the forward reaction control system can be clearly seen, as can the individual insulating tiles on the nose and fuselage.

Right: The orbiter's main engines are among the most efficient power units ever produced, developing a thrust of up to 450,000 pounds (204,000 kilograms) for a weight of only 6,700 pounds (3,000 kilograms). They burn a mixture of liquid hydrogen and liquid oxygen, which are stored in the huge external tank.

Left: Test firing of the shuttle main engines at NASA's National Space Technology Laboratories in Bay St Louis, Mississippi. The clouds are of steam, produced by the combustion of the hydrogen and oxygen propellants.

Below right: One of the orbiter's three main engines being guided into position in the tail. Although the engines were designed for a long life (at least 50 take-offs), they have proved troublesome and will undoubtedly need replacing more frequently.

Above: Technicians at work sticking tiles on the fuselage of orbiter *Columbia*. When the job is complete, some 34,000 tiles will form a heat shield over the craft. This shield will protect the orbiter's airframe and the astronauts inside from the heat developed as the craft re-enters the Earth's atmosphere when returning from orbit.

Above: The flight deck of the shuttle orbiter, with most instruments and displays in position. It looks much like the flight deck of a large airliner, but differs in having three video screens. The pilots can call up onto these screens information about any of the shuttle's extensive flight and navigation systems.

Above: The prototype orbiter *Enterprise* flies piggy back on a converted Boeing 747 jumbo jet on its first manned test flight in 1977. In later flights *Enterprise* separates from its carrier jet and carries out several successful runway landings. This series of approach and landing tests confirms the aerodynamic performance of this unique space vehicle.

Top right: The shuttle orbiter is hauled up vertically in the Vehicle Assembly Building ready to be attached to its external tank. This picture shows clearly the heat-resistant tiles on the underside. Here they are coated black and are thickest in order to withstand temperatures of over 700°C.

Right: The shuttle orbiter is being lowered into position onto its external fuel tank and side rocket booster in the Vehicle Assembly Building. When in position, the shuttle assembly will be complete and ready to roll out to the launch pad.

3. THE SHUTTLE ASTRONAUTS

In the early days of manned space flight astronauts all had to be relatively young, in superb physical condition, with lightning reactions and be very experienced jet pilots. First man on the Moon, Neil Armstrong, for example, was typical. He joined the astronaut corps in 1962, aged 32. He had flown 78 combat missions in the Korean War and spent 1,100 hours as a test pilot testing supersonic planes as well as the X-15 rocket plane. At the age of 39 he was stepping down onto the Moon and making a giant leap for mankind.

Things have changed a lot since then. Age certainly is no longer a barrier. John Young, at the age of 51, commanded the first shuttle flight in 1981, and in 1983 returned to space on the ninth shuttle mission for a record six times. Russian cosmonauts in their 50s are also still coping well with the rigors of space flight.

Another significant departure from early practise is that people other than career astronauts can now make it into space. Germany's Ulf Merbold is typical of the new breed. He is a scientist, who flew on the Spacelab mission after just a few months' training. McDonnell Douglas engineer Charles Walker became another temporary astronaut when he flew on mission 41-D in 1984.

A further notable change in recent years has been the emergence of the woman astronaut. NASA has had several women in training since the late 1970s, among them Dr Sally Ride, who became the first American woman in space in 1983. She was the third woman in the world to orbit the Earth. Russian cosmonaut Valentina Tereshkova was the first, as long ago as 1963. Her fellow countrywoman Svetlana Savitskaya became the second in 1982, and indeed returned to orbit two years later.

The Training

John Young and Robert Crippen, who flew the first shuttle mission, are astronauts, one might say, of the old school. They form part of a group of pilot-astronauts whose main task is to fly the orbiter. Other career astronauts are classified as mission specialists and payload specialists. They are responsible for aspects of particular missions or for particular payloads upon those missions.

The different responsibilities of the astronauts naturally affect their training. The pilot-astronauts, for example, keep their hand in flying jets. They spend a great deal of time in the shuttle mission simulator. This is, inside, an identical replica of the orbiter flight deck. All the instruments and controls are 'live', in that they react in exactly the same way as the real ones would in flight.

The pilot-astronauts regularly go over the procedures for a forthcoming mission in simulations with mission control at Houston. They also prepare for emergencies by learning to cope with simulated equipment and engine failures.

The other crew members, the mission and payload specialists, need not necessarily know how to fly the orbiter. Their training will therefore center on rehearsing for their own particular roles in orbit. They may well also use simulators to practice, for example, using the orbiter's remote manipulator arm. This is often used to launch or retrieve satellites. Payload specialists are usually scientists or engineers familiar with the payload to be carried or with experiments to be performed. Missions involving Spacelab require the largest number of payload specialists since the experimental workload is heavy.

G-forces

Some aspects of training, however, are shared by all the astronauts to prepare them for the extraordinary happenings and sensations that occur during lift-off and when traveling in space. During lift-off and ascent into orbit the acceleration of

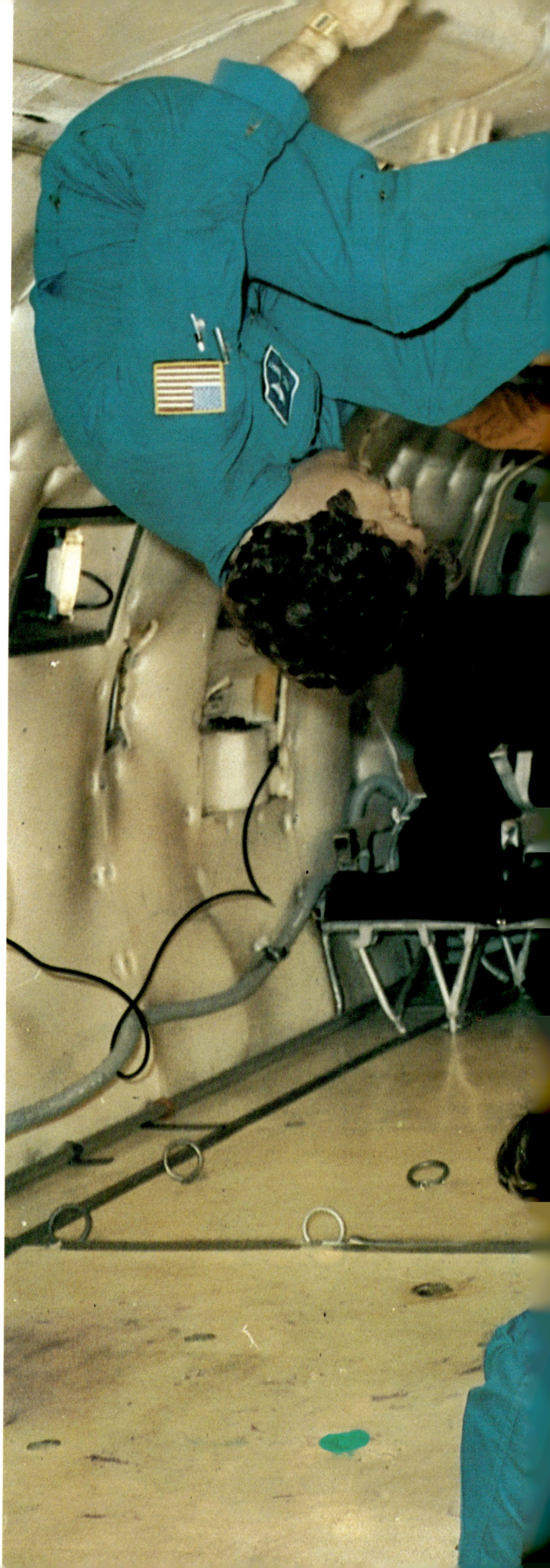

Astronauts Anna Fisher and Frederick Hauck float weightless for a few minutes during a zero-gravity training session on board a KC-135 aircraft. To simulate zero gravity, the plane flies up and over in a tight arc, causing the people inside to free fall.

DIV.
NASA, MSC,
TEXAS

the rockets forces them back in their seats. They become up to three times heavier than usual. We say they pull 3Gs (1G referring to the normal pull of gravity). In training they can experience similar G-forces by being whirled round in a centrifuge. This machine sets up centrifugal forces on the body as it spins rapidly in a circle.

By contrast, when astronauts have entered orbit they appear not to have any weight at all. They are effectively in zero-gravity, in a weightless condition. It is not so easy to train for this on Earth. The astronauts can experience weightlessness very briefly by flying in a specially arcing plane. They can experience something similar in a water immersion facility, such as that at Houston. This is a huge water tank in which astronauts 'dive' in suits similar to spacesuits. The suits are weighted so that the astronauts neither rise nor sink – they are in a state of neutral buoyancy. In the tank they can not only get the feel of weightlessness but also rehearse operations they will need to carry out in orbit, particularly spacewalking. The water immersion facility is large enough to accommodate full-scale mock-ups of space hardware such as the shuttle cargo bay and the space telescope.

The Shuttle Spacesuit

When the astronauts go spacewalking, of course, they will need to wear a spacesuit to protect them from the hostile, airless world of space. Early spacesuits were developments of the pressure suits worn by high-flying pilots. They were supplied with oxygen through a tube called an umbilical, which was connected to their spacecraft's life-support system. This arrangement was cumbersome and was potentially lethal if the tube was punctured.

The shuttle spacesuit is much safer in that it is self-contained, the oxygen being provided from a backpack. Like earlier versions the suit is made up of layers. Next to the skin is a pair of water-cooled long pants. Water circulates through these to keep the astronaut cool. Then there is a pressure suit supplied with oxygen for the astronaut to breathe. A tough outer insulating layer of metal and plastic completes the suit, providing protection from heat, cold and dangerous cosmic radiation.

The shuttle astronauts have a further advantage over their earlier colleagues. They have a jet-propelled backpack to help them move around in space. It is a development of a unit flown on Skylab in the 1970s, and is known as a manned maneuvering unit (MMU). The spacesuited astronaut backs into the MMU and latches onto it. He controls the device by two hand controllers, which fire combinations of gas jets to allow movement in any direction.

Left: The two astronauts chosen to pioneer space shuttle travel, John Young (left) and Robert Crippen. Young is a space veteran of the Gemini and Apollo eras. Crippen is a rookie, who has yet to fly in space.

Below: Commander Young and pilot Crippen spend much of the preflight period training in the cockpit of the craft they will fly into space, orbiter *Columbia*. Here they are going through a detailed check list of operations to be performed during a simulation with Mission Control. The 'thumbs-up' sign indicates that all is going according to plan.

Above: It is the morning of April 12, 1981, two hours before the scheduled lift-off of *Columbia* on its maiden voyage. Young and Crippen are enjoying the astronaut's traditional steak and eggs breakfast. The tension they feel is reflected in their faces. They will be piloting a totally new spacecraft, which has never before been tested in space. They, like everyone else at NASA, are wondering: will it fly?

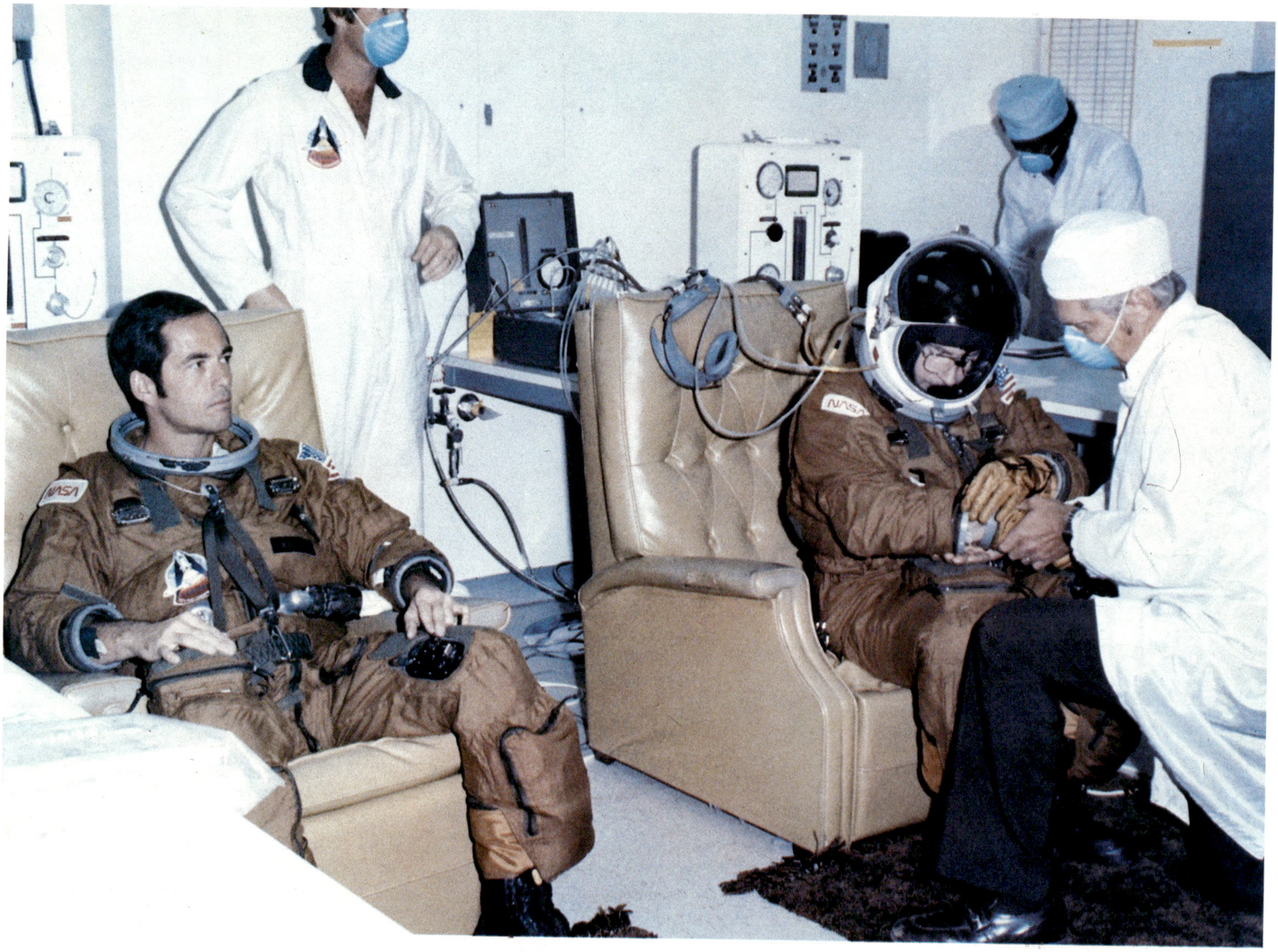

Above: With the countdown proceeding smoothly, astronauts Crippen and Young get suited up in the Operations and Checkout Building at the Kennedy Space Center. Next they are transported to the launch pad at Complex 39, and installed in *Columbia*. The hatch is closed and all service personnel withdraw. As the astronauts busy themselves with last-minute checks, the final minutes of the countdown tick away.

Opposite: Watched by more than a million people, Crippen and Young in *Columbia* rocket from the launch pad in a spectacular blaze of flame, steam and smoke. Their maiden lift-off is perfect. So too, 54½ hours later, is their touchdown. *Columbia* is hailed by NASA as a 'magnificent flying machine'.

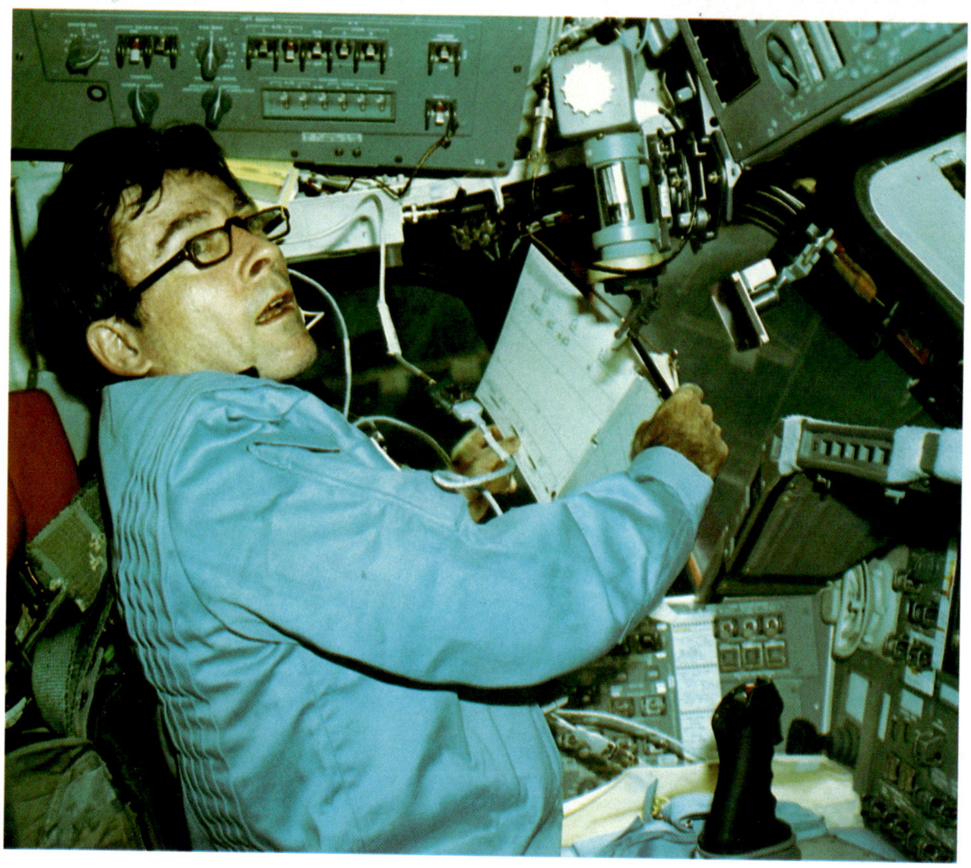

Right: Up in orbit on the historic first shuttle flight, Commander Young catches up with some paper work. On the first few shuttle flights the crew act very much as test pilots, helping to iron out problems in the shuttle systems and operating procedures.

SPACE SHUTTLE

Left: Astronaut Gordon Fullerton tries out a shuttle spacesuit in the zero-gravity conditions of an arcing aircraft. The shuttle spacesuit is unlike the suits used on previous orbital missions, such as Skylab, because it is self-contained. Skylab suits, for example, were supplied with air by tube from the spacecraft's life-support system.

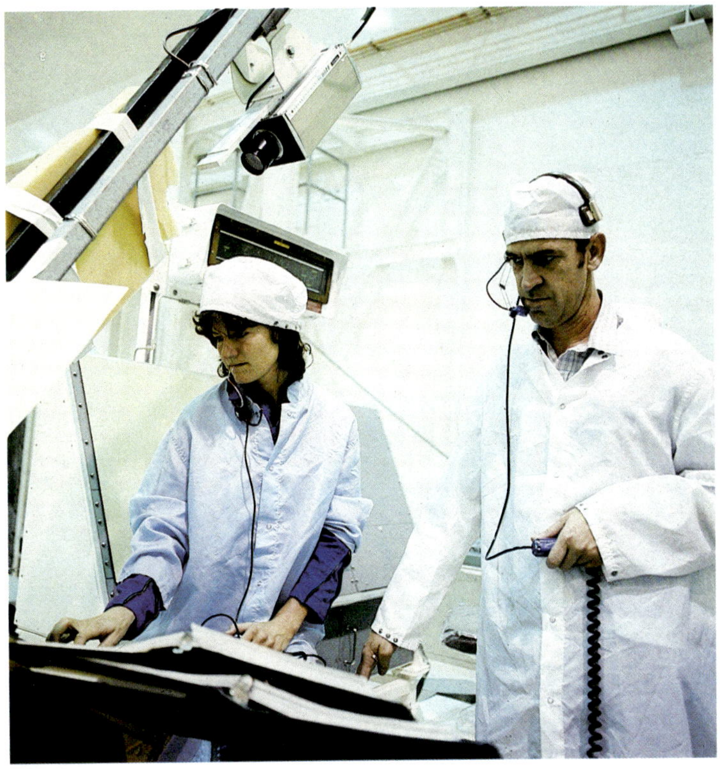

Right: Astronauts Sally Ride and John Fabian taking part in a simulation of operations they will later carry out in space. Sally Ride becomes the first American woman astronaut when she flies on the seventh shuttle flight.

Below: Shuttle pilots spend much of their training time at the controls of the shuttle mission simulator at the Johnson Space Center at Houston, Texas. The simulator has identical controls and instrumentation to the real craft, and they react exactly as they would in real flight. The astronauts are Jack Lousma (left), who first went into space in Skylab, and Gordon Fullerton, pilot for the third shuttle flight.

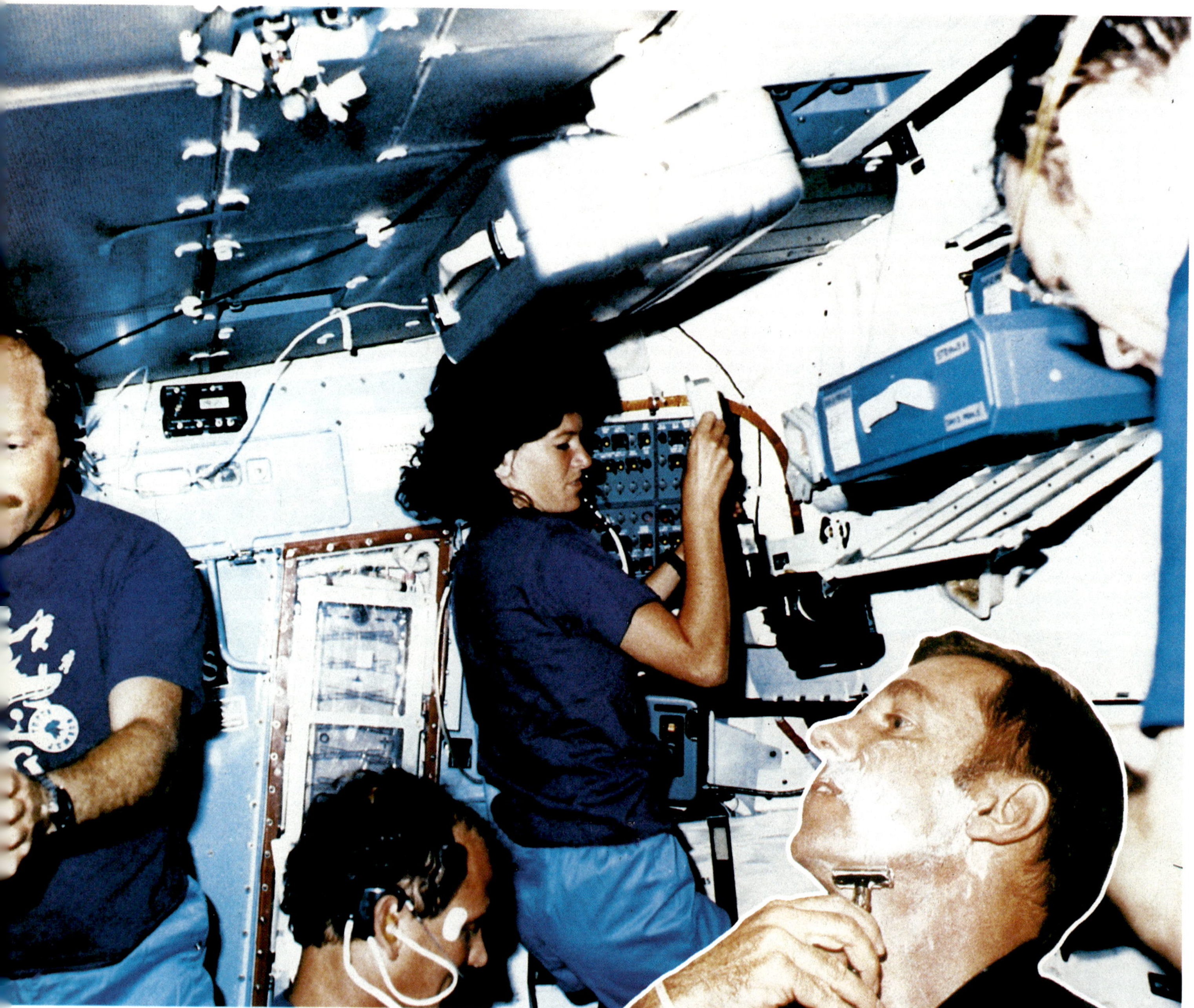

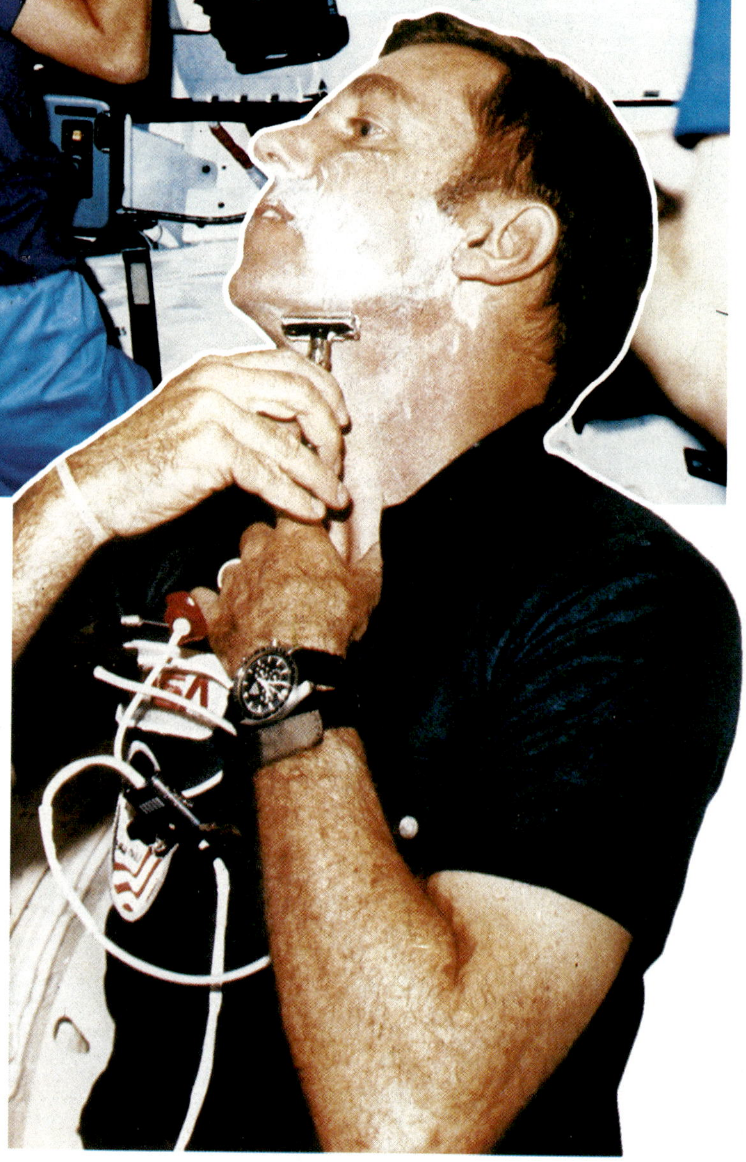

Above: Up in space in the orbiter *Challenger,* Commander Robert Crippen snaps this picture of his four fellow astronauts preparing a between-meals snack. It is the seventh flight of the shuttle, on which Sally Ride becomes the first American woman in space.

Right: Shuttle astronauts 'wash and brush up' in a toilet compartment in the mid-deck of the orbiter. Here astronaut Joe Engle is seen shaving. There is plenty of water for washing and drinking aboard. It is supplied by the fuel cells that produce the shuttle's electricity.

Opposite: Also on the seventh shuttle flight, pilot Fred Hauck is seen exercising on a treadmill device. By carrying out such exercise regularly, astronauts can counter the effect of weightlessness on their bodies, which tends to make their muscles waste away. The effect becomes progressively worse the longer the astronauts remain in orbit.

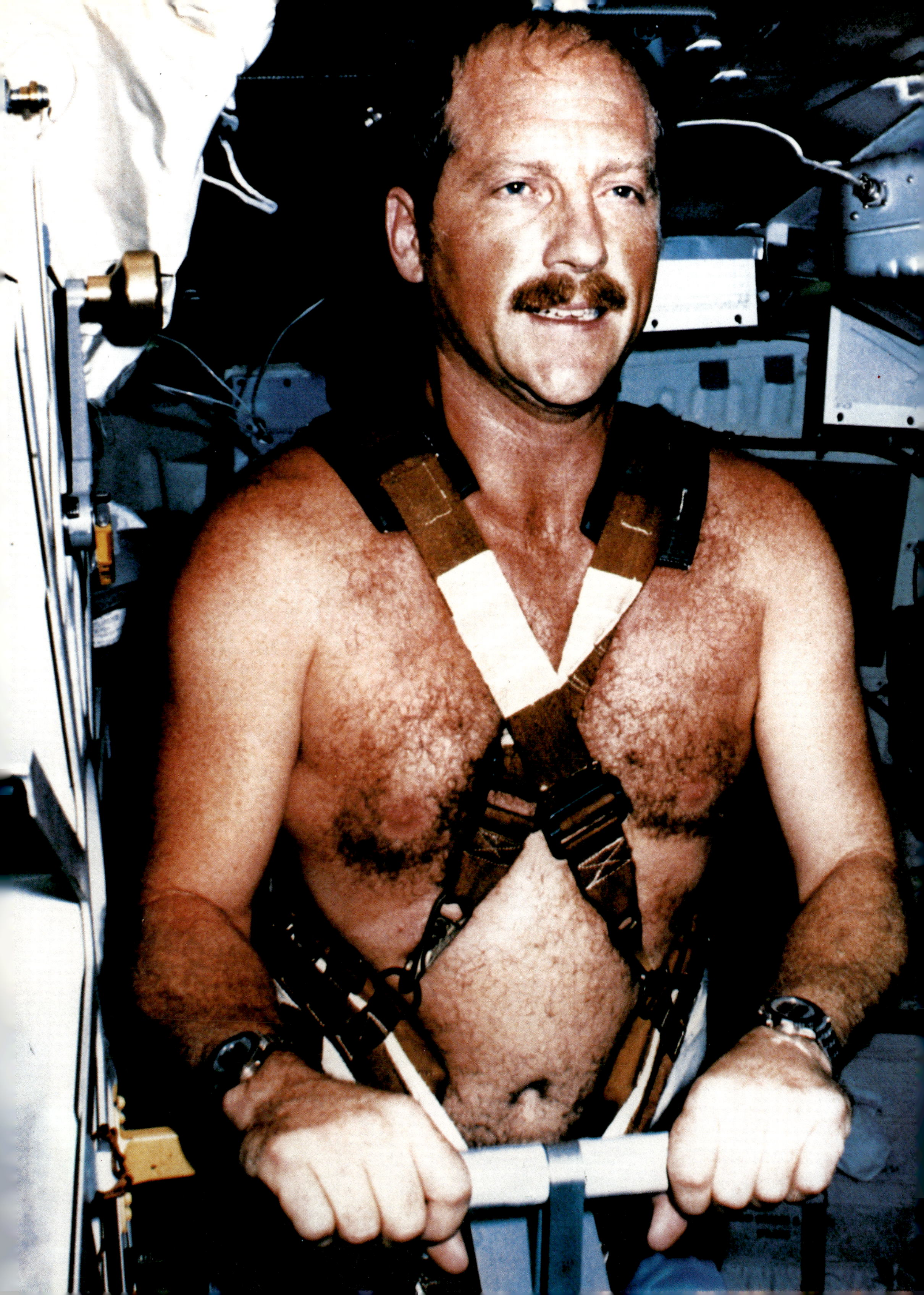

Left: On board orbiter *Challenger* during the sixth shuttle mission, astronauts Story Musgrave (left) and Donald Peterson test the new shuttle spacesuits. They are seen floating in *Challenger's* cargo bay and for safety are tethered to slide wires running along the edge.

Above: When retrieving or repairing satellites, spacesuited shuttle astronauts carry out operations with the assistance of the shuttle's remote manipulator arm. On shuttle mission 41-B in February 1984 Bruce McCandless rehearses recovery procedures.

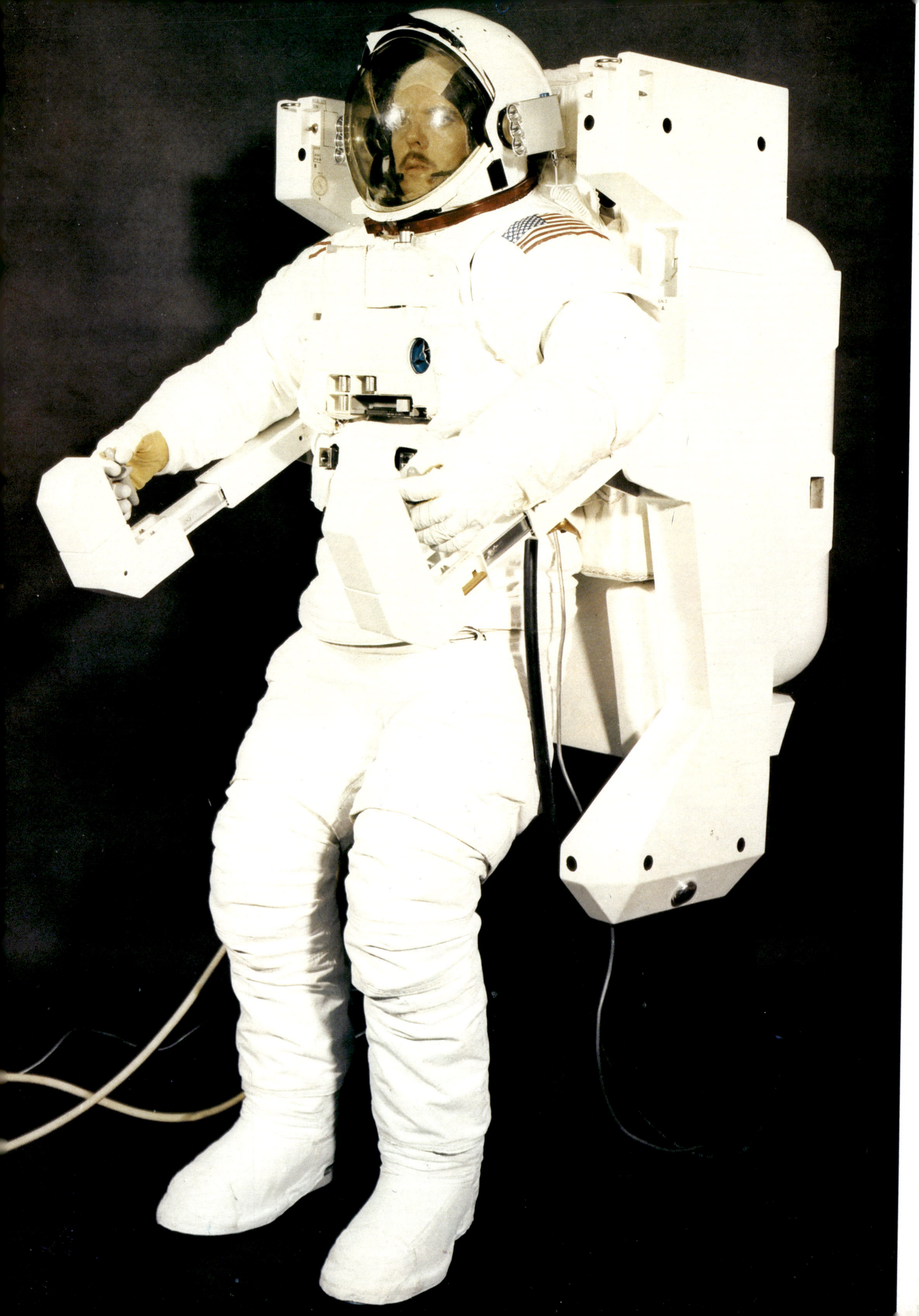

Left: Shuttle astronauts are able to move about in space much more easily than their predecessors thanks to the manned maneuvering unit. This is a 'Buck Rogers' type flying machine which the astronauts attach to their bodies. They move about by firing gas jets in the appropriate direction.

Right: Bruce McCandless tests the manned maneuvering unit in orbit in February 1984 to make the first untethered spacewalk. In this picture he has reached a distance of 300 feet (90 metres) from the orbiter and is about to jet back. The unit performs well and is ready for use on the satellite recovery missions that follow.

Below: When astronauts become marooned in orbit on crippled shuttle craft, they can be rescued in this ball device. It is the personal rescue enclosure, which is made of the same material as the shuttle suit and has its own life-support and communications systems. Astronauts are zipped into the ball, which is then carried through space to the rescue craft.

Bottom right: A demonstration model of the personal rescue enclosure, showing an astronaut inside. Some 34 inches across, it is not the height of comfort, but it does provide short-term protection from the deadly space environment.

4. IN ORBIT OPERATION

Compared with earlier space launching vehicles – ordinary rockets – the shuttle has many advantages. First and foremost it has a huge cargo capacity. It can carry into orbit payloads the size of a railroad car. It can comfortably carry several satellites at once, and still have room for a number of experiment canisters in between. These canister payloads are known as Getaway Specials. They offer industrial and educational establishments an opportunity of participating in space research at a reasonable cost.

Another great advantage the shuttle has over ordinary rocket launch vehicles is that it is a manned craft. The crew can literally place a satellite into space and check that it is working properly before leaving. If the satellite malfunctions at this stage – a not uncommon occurrence – then it can be brought back to Earth for attention.

Satellite launchings from the shuttle are still not totally reliable, however. In February 1984 two expensive communications satellites were lost after launch from *Challenger* on the tenth shuttle mission. The fault lay not with the shuttle launch system, however, but with the booster rockets that should have lifted the satellite into high orbit. Boosters are needed for high-orbit satellites, because the effective ceiling of the shuttle is only about 600 miles (1,000 kilometers).

The Shuttle Crane

Most satellites are launched from pods within the orbiter's payload bay, but some are launched with the help of a remote-controlled 'crane'. This is a 50-foot (15-meter) long arm fixed to the interior of the bay. It is known as the remote manipulator arm. It is made in several sections connected by flexible joints and is powered by electric motors. It can be moved in any direction by means of remote hand controllers located on a console on the aft flight deck of the orbiter. The astronauts controlling the device can view it through windows looking into the cargo bay and overhead. In fact they carry out all payload launch operations from the same console.

The remote manipulator arm, first tested on the second shuttle flight, has already proved invaluable. It was used on the eleventh shuttle flight to capture the satellite known as Solar Max after attempts by shuttle astronauts to do so had failed.

Shuttle Housekeeping

The time astronauts spend in orbit is very limited, and they have to get through a heavy workload. This work is precisely regulated according to a strict time schedule worked out beforehand. So are the periods allotted to what might be called the 'housekeeping' activities of eating, sleeping, washing and so on.

The living quarters of the shuttle are on the mid-deck. They are not very spacious because so much equipment must be fitted in. They include a kitchen, or galley unit, sleep stations, a 'bathroom' and storage lockers. The galley unit houses an oven, pantry, trays, and water dispensers. The latter are used to inject water into dehydrated foods and prepare them for eating. Many of the foods the astronauts eat are dehydrated. Some are frozen or canned, while others are in their natural form. They may need to be warmed in the oven before eating.

Compared with their earlier colleagues, the shuttle astronauts enjoy an appetizing and varied diet. Gone are the days of tasteless goo from toothpaste-tube-like containers. Shuttle meals are now much more like those served in airliners. The astronauts can select a variety of prepackaged meals, having perhaps for breakfast scrambled eggs, bran flakes and orange; for lunch, corned beef, asparagus and peas; and for dinner smoked turkey, mixed vegetables and strawberries. A variety of between-meals snacks are also

This unique view of orbiter *Challenger* was taken by an automatic camera on the shuttle pallet satellite in June 1983. Visible in the cargo bay of the orbiter are the cradles from which communications satellites have been launched, and an experiments pallet for NASA.

available. The daily menu is designed to provide an energy intake of about 3,000 calories. Meal preparation time is about 20 minutes.

On missions with a large crew, such as Spacelab, the astronauts generally have to eat in shifts. They also have to sleep in shifts too. There is normally room for four astronauts to sleep – three in bunk 'beds' and one hanging on the wall. They sleep zipped up in sleeping bags to prevent them floating away.

The shuttle 'bathroom' is quite cramped, being a compartment tucked behind the galley. It has a wash basin and mirror and a flush toilet. Unlike on Earth, the toilet is flushed with air not water. The 'flushing' air stream is needed to remove the body wastes, which would otherwise, in zero-gravity, just float unpleasantly about.

Another thing that limits space in the mid-deck area of the orbiter is the presence of the airlock. Astronauts use the airlock when they have to go spacewalking, or perform extra-vehicular activity (EVA). The airlock is a cylindrical chamber from which the air can be removed. It has two doors, one from the mid-deck area and another that opens into the cargo bay. In the airlock the astronauts put on their spacesuits, which are stored there. They then depressurize the airlock and open the door to the payload bay. They reverse the procedure when they return from space. The manned maneuvering units they sometimes use are stored just inside the payload bay.

Laboratory in Space

As well as launching satellites, the shuttle carries more ambitious payloads into orbit. One of the most important is Spacelab. This is a fully fitted out scientific and engineering laboratory, which was designed and built in Europe by members of the European Space Agency. Spacelab made its debut in November 1983 on the ninth shuttle mission. On this occasion there were six astronauts on board, including West Germany's Ulf Merbold, one of the payload specialists with particular responsibilities for the 70 or so experiments carried.

Spacelab may be flown in one of several configurations. The main unit is a cylindrical pressurized module, fully equipped with ovens, apparatus, electronics equipment, microscopes and so on. The scientist-astronauts work there in 'shirt-sleeve' comfort, traveling to it through a pressurized tunnel connected to the airlock. Often an unpressurized platform, or pallet, is flown with the laboratory module. On it are mounted instruments and apparatus that need to be exposed to the space environment. The Spacelab astronauts carry out experiments in many fields, including astronomy, physics, engineering, Earth resources, meteorology, space processing, life sciences and space medicine. One urgent investigation carried out is on space sickness, a condition that affects the majority of astronauts for the first few days in orbit. But the solution of this and other space medical problems probably requires longer investigation than Spacelab allows. It may have to wait until permanent space stations are built, probably out of modules like Spacelab.

Left: Launching satellites is one of the shuttle's main tasks. Here an Indonesian communications satellite, *Palapa B*, is ejected from the cargo bay and starts its journey into high Earth orbit.

Above, main picture: After a satellite has been launched, the shuttle astronauts check it out, and afterwards move their craft some distance away. Then they ignite a solid rocket motor attached to the satellite, which is needed to propel it into the correct orbit.

Above, inset: On the eighth shuttle mission the payload-specialist astronauts practice launching procedures using the remote manipulator arm. In this test they are lifting a payload flight test article from the cargo bay. As in earlier tests, the remote manipulator arm, which is built by Canada, performs perfectly.

Above: the shuttle is able to launch not only satellites into orbit, but also space probes to more remote destinations in the solar system. This picture shows the launch from low Earth orbit of a probe to Jupiter. A powerful booster rocket is attached to the spacecraft and accelerates at a speed of 25,000 mph (40,000 kilometers an hour) so that it can escape from the Earth's gravity.

Right: Astronaut Gordon Fullerton looks out of the aft window on *Columbia's* flight deck during the third shuttle mission. The instrument and control console there is operated by payload-specialist astronauts when carrying out payload operations with the remote manipulator arm.

Below: As well as launching satellites and probes, the shuttle often carries a variety of experiments into orbit on pallets, or in canisters which are open to the space environment. Sometimes experiments packages are lifted out of the cargo bay by the remote manipulator arm, as here.

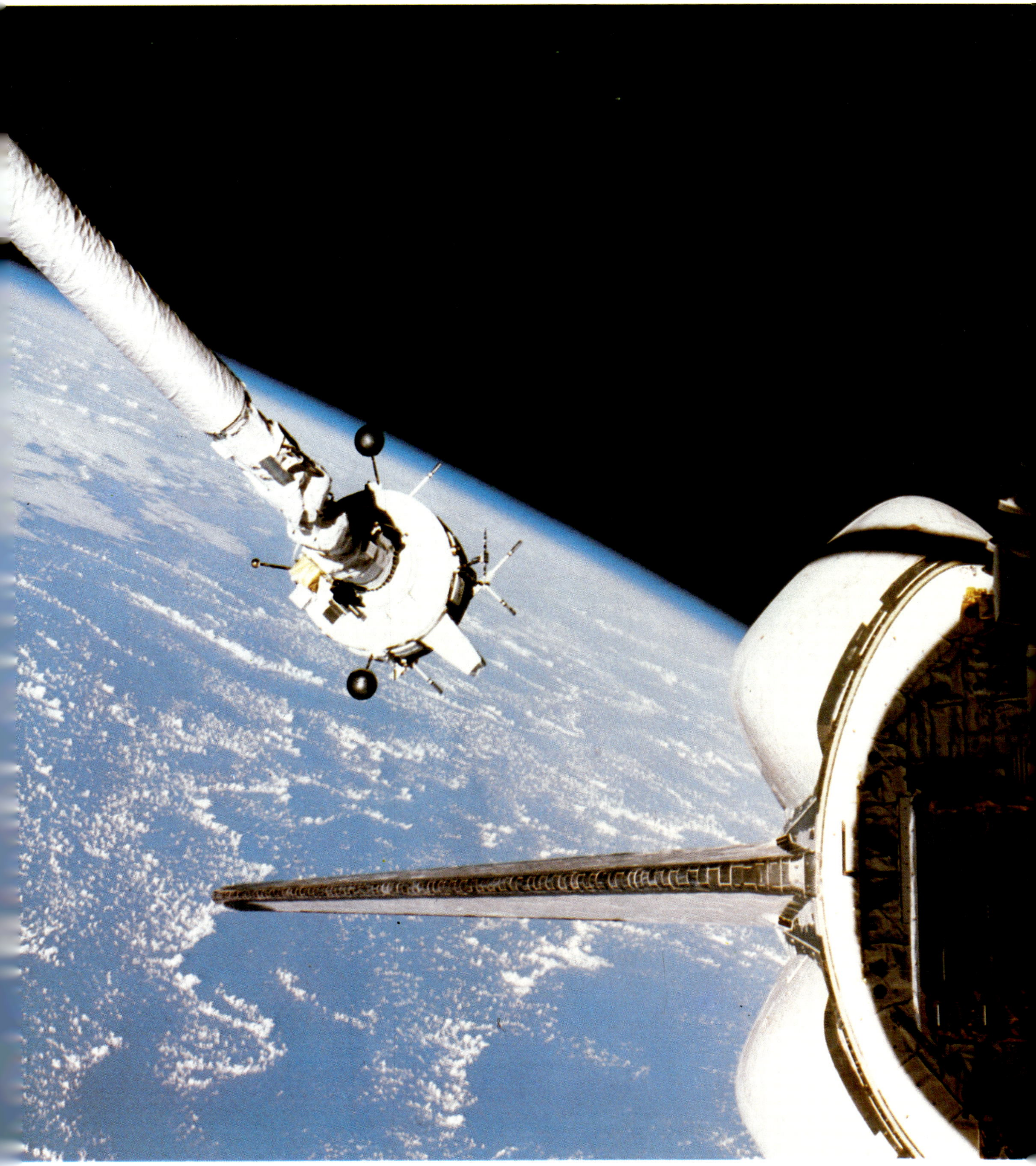

DONNELL
OUGLAS
western union
HUGHES
WESTAR VI

Left: In this rehearsal for a forthcoming satellite capture mission, Bruce McCandless moves in to lock with an attachment on the shuttle pallet satellite. This formed part of the 41-B shuttle mission in February 1984 in which McCandless and fellow crew member Robert Stewart tested the manned maneuvering units in orbit for the first time.

Above: The maneuver McCandless practiced for was the capture of the satellite known as Solar Max. On the next flight two months later, George Nielson tries out the same procedure on the real satellite. But he is unsuccessful. Eventually the satellite is captured with the help of the remote manipulator arm.

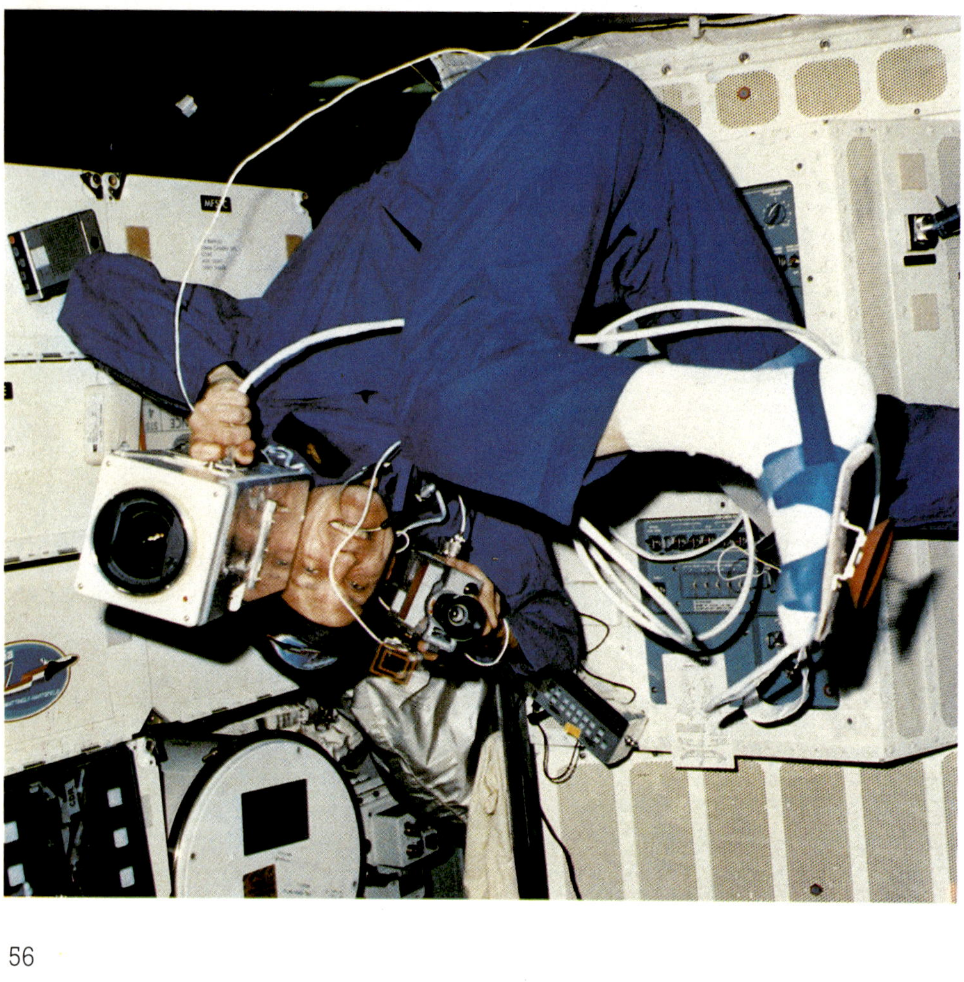

Top left: The shuttle crew has a rota for meal preparation, which usually involves adding water to dehydrated items and putting containers in the oven. Here, astronaut Gordon Fullerton is in charge. He is holding a beverage in a concertina-type dispenser, while other meal packages are stuck to doors and trays by Velcro strips.

Bottom left: Floating in the mid-deck area of *Columbia*, astronaut Thomas Mattingly demonstrates his versatility by handling two cameras at once. Note his special footwear, which has suction cups to enable him to anchor himself to a surface. They are not standard issue for the astronauts.

Above: Only two of the shuttle crew have responsibility for piloting the orbiter on each mission. The others are concerned with payload operations and 'housekeeping', for example, meal preparations. Here Vance Brand (left) and Robert Overmeyer occupy respectively the commander and pilot seats as they go over flight procedures prior to re-entry.

Left: One fear on early shuttle flights is the possibility of loss of heat-shield tiles from the critical area. If this happens, will it cause the airframe beneath to be damaged? As the picture taken on the very first flight shows, tiles are missing from the tail unit. Fortunately this causes no problem during re-entry, and the tiles on the underside – a critical area – remain intact.

Right: However, tile damage in a critical area may occur. So NASA has prepared a tile repair kit which astronauts can use to repair the heat shield in orbit. Here it is being demonstrated by astronaut William Lenoir at the Johnson Space Center in Houston.

Left: One of the most important payloads carried by the shuttle is the European-built space laboratory, Spacelab. It is pictured here in the open cargo bay of orbiter *Columbia* on its maiden flight in November 1983. This picture, taken through one of the windows of the aft flight deck, shows in the foreground the docking tunnel, which leads to the cylindrical laboratory modules.

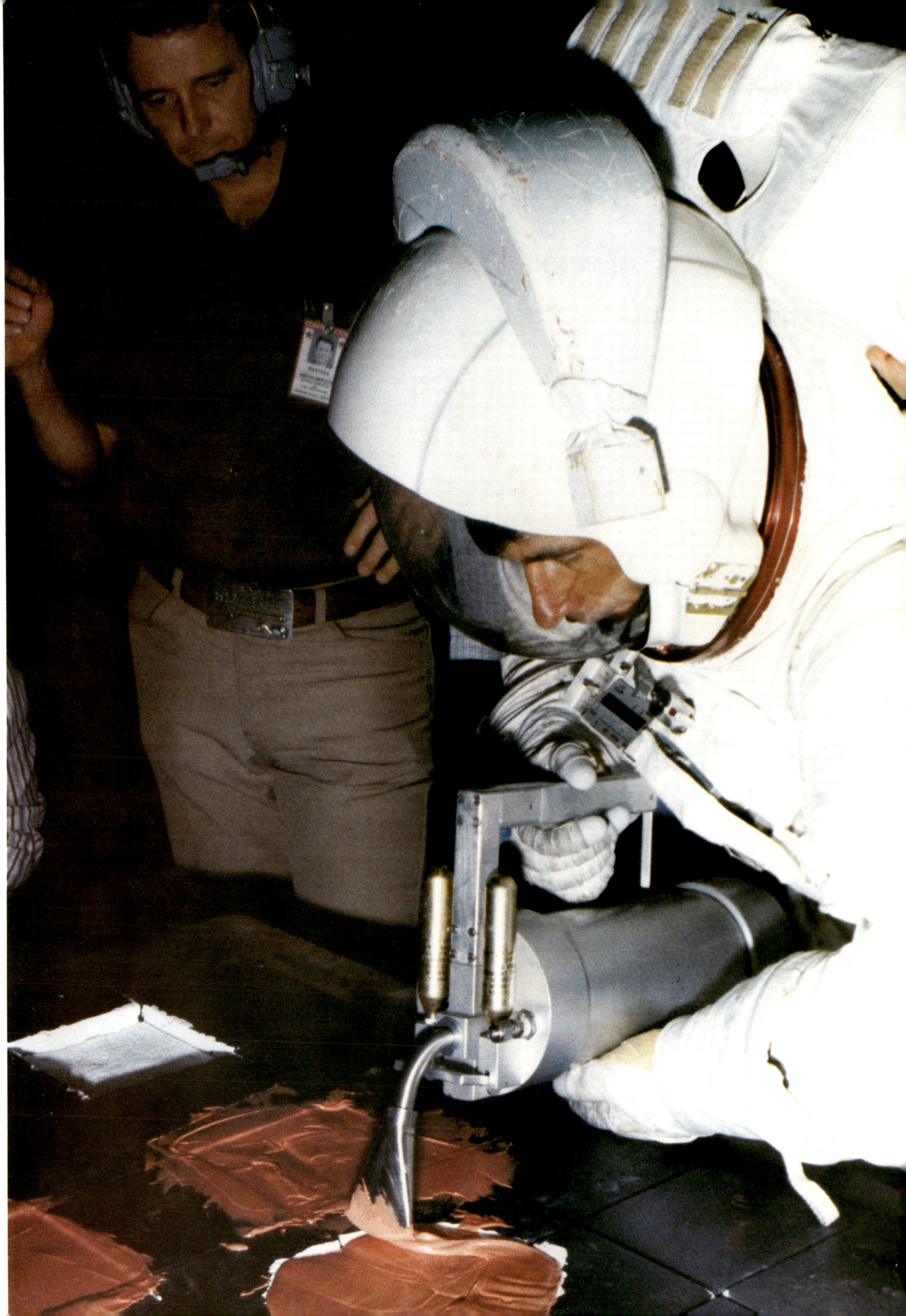

Left, inset top: Spacelab astronauts confer over one of the 70 or so experiments they perform in space on the first Spacelab mission. Among the six astronauts is a West German scientist, Ulf Merbold, who becomes the first European to take part in an American space mission.

Left, inset bottom: Shuttle astronauts take the opportunity of photographing the Earth from orbit through the overhead windows on the orbiter flight deck. The first shuttle crew snap this dramatic view of the towering Himalayas from an altitude of about 150 miles (240 kilometers).

Above: On major scientific missions large volumes of data are generated. Here on the first Spacelab mission, astronaut Brewster Shaw is reviewing the data on a print-out from the teleprinter on *Columbia's* mid-deck. The on-board computing facilities allow initial analysis of experimental data, which proves a boon to the scientists conducting the experiments.

Left, main picture: The astronauts on shuttle mission capture this dramatic cloudscape over Africa. The land some 150 miles (240 kilometers) below is hidden in a haze caused by agricultural burning.

5. TOWARDS TOMORROW

What does the future hold for space exploration in the decades and even centuries ahead? If the achievements of the last quarter century of the Space Age are anything to go by, the future seems rosy. The advent of the space shuttle has seen to this. It provides a reliable means of transporting people and equipment into orbit at reasonable cost. It should prove the means by which the dreams of generations of space enthusiasts will become reality.

These people have visualized space stations, power satellites, space factories, orbiting communications complexes, Moon bases, space colonies and missions to Mars. All these things should now be within our grasp – eventually.

Experimental Space Stations

Now that the space shuttle transportation system has become fully operational, the establishment of a permanent space station has become one of NASA's main objectives. They are aiming to have one in orbit by the early 1990s.

The benefits to be gained from a long-term presence in space were well documented by the American Skylab mission in 1973/74. Skylab was an experimental space station made up of items of hardware left over from the Apollo Moon-landing programme. The main part was a Saturn V rocket casing, which was converted into a spacious living and work area. Other pieces were added, such as instrument clusters, docking ports and solar panels, making it into a 120-foot (36-meter) long, 200,000-pound (90,000-kilogram) unit.

Over a 10-month period three teams of three astronauts were ferried up to Skylab in surplus Apollo spacecraft and in turn spent respectively 28, 59 and 84 days in orbit. The mission was a spectacular success, beating all space endurance records, and proving that human beings can survive long periods in space without coming to any harm. The scientific value of the Skylab mission was impressive, particularly in the field of solar physics. In just a few months' observation from Skylab, scientists acquired more information about the Sun than they could have gained from centuries of observation from the ground.

Skylab, however, was a one-off space station, unrepeatable and unable to be developed. Elsewhere in the sky, however, a longer term space station program was underway. It was being conducted by the Russians. They launched their first experimental space station, Salyut 1, in 1971, and sent teams of cosmonauts to visit it in Soyuz ferry craft. Over the years they have launched a series of improved Salyut craft, culminating with the present Salyut 7 in 1982.

While the United States has concentrated on bringing the space shuttle into operation, the Russians have continued to refine their space station hardware and operating procedures. In particular they have achieved some remarkable space endurance records. In 1982 two cosmonauts remained in orbit for 211 days, four months longer than any American astronaut. The Russians have also achieved great success with re-supplying Salyut by means of robot ferry craft called Progress. They have also automatically docked extra modules with Salyut to increase the size of the space station.

This space station of the not-too-distant future has been suggested by builders of the space shuttle, Rockwell International. Like many concepts it features a station made up of connected cylindrical modules. It generates the electricity it needs by means of large panels of solar cells. The station will be kept permanently manned and serviced regularly by orbiters of an expanded shuttle fleet.

The Modular Station

Intensive planning is now going on at NASA establishments to finalize a design for a practical space station for a decade hence. This station will not be a 'one-off' exercise like Skylab, but a design capable of expansion and modification for a variety of roles.

One of its major roles will be as a scientific base, where scientists and engineers will experiment in the unique condition of zero-gravity and high vacuum unobtainable on Earth. They will also conduct experiments in the biological sciences, particularly in space medicine. Experiments already carried out in orbit have shown that better constructional and electronics materials can be produced in space, together with purer vaccines. This should lead to the establishment of space factories to produce such materials on an industrial scale.

Another major role for the space station will be as a satellite service center. It will have facilities for retrieving and repairing satellites in orbit, something that the shuttle has already demonstrated is practical. It could later be developed into a spaceport to handle spacecraft traveling between the Earth and bases on the Moon and maybe even Mars.

The shuttle will play a critical role in the construction of the 1990s space station. The station will be assembled from a number of standard-size modules designed to fit into the cargo bay of the shuttle orbiter. Spacelab can be seen as a prototype for such a unit. The modules will be fitted out with the appropriate equipment during manufacture on Earth. Some will act as living quarters, some as laboratories and some as stores for food and propellants. The modules will then be ferried into orbit on a series of shuttle flights. The shuttles will also carry up tubes fitted with docking ports.

In orbit, typically about 250 miles (400 kilometers) high, the modules and tubes will be fitted together to form the space station. This will be done by a team of astronaut-technicians in manned maneuvering units, with the assistance of the shuttle orbiter's remote manipulating arm. Solar arrays, also ferried up by shuttle, will be attached to provide electrical power for the station. It is envisaged that astronauts will spend about 3 months at a time in the station.

Large Space Structures

In time the modular space station will take on a new role, as a construction base for massive space engineering projects. One of the most likely projects is the satellite power station. This will need to be built in stationary orbit, some 22,300 miles (36,000 kilometers) high. At this height it will appear stationary as seen from the Earth, and will be in the sun virtually the whole time.

The power station will harness the energy in sunlight either by means of solar cells or by means of reflectors. To capture enough energy, the solar cell arrays or reflectors will have to be huge – many miles across. The energy collected will be converted into microwaves, in which form they can be transmitted efficiently to Earth. There they will be converted into electrical power. There are no fundamental theoretical problems about such a project – the real problem is one of scale, for some 100,000 tons of material will be required.

Cities in Space

About five times this amount of material will be required for a prototype of the first city or colony in space. Several designs have been suggested for such a city, which could hold up to 10,000 people. One design houses the population in the outer tube of a wheel-like structure, or torus. Another consists of pairs of connected cylinders.

The city will be built in far-off orbit some 240,000 miles (390,000 kilometers) away from the Earth and at an equal distance from the Moon. The materials needed to build the city will come from minerals mined on the Moon and smelted in space.

This vision of huge colonies floating in space and Moon mining bases may seem fantastic to us at present. But who would be rash enough to say that they will never happen? Remember the Age of Space has hardly begun.

Left: This space shuttle is on a long duration scientific mission, lasting up to four months. Normal shuttle missions last for only a week or two. For long stays in orbit on-board power resources on the orbiter are inadequate, so it has attached to it a power module, which generates electricity from solar panels.

Above: By the end of this century this could be a typical scene in orbit as space engineering projects get underway. Astronaut-engineers with remote-control robot devices are seen here constructing a mammoth solar power station.

Right: Space stations provide the springboard for a variety of other space structures. Among them is the solar power station. This particular power station consists of a solar cell array 30 miles (50 kilometers) long. It beams energy down to Earth in the form of microwaves.

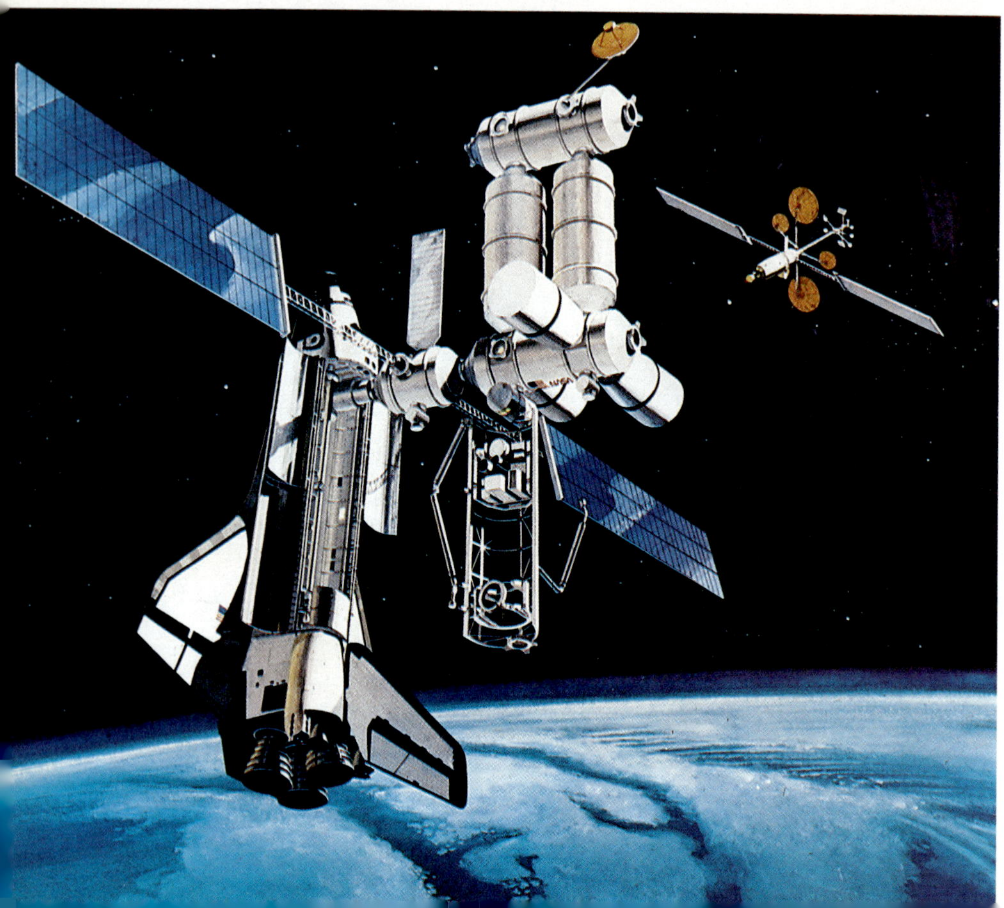

Above: The microwave energy beamed down to Earth from solar power satellites is gathered by a huge antenna on the ground several miles across. The energy is then converted into electricity and fed into the national grid. Normal farming activities are carried out on the ground beneath the antenna.

Left: This NASA space station of the 1990s provides permanent living accommodation for a crew of eight or more. Its various types of modules provide a pressurized environment for living, working and recreation. Unpressurized structures provide 'garage' space for orbital transfer vehicles which carry satellites into higher orbit.

Below: This Lockheed space station of next century features a rotating living quarters module. Rotation of the module sets up centrifugal forces which imitate the pull of gravity. Astronauts find life more comfortable in this artificial gravity environment.

LUNOX ISA

Above: The Moon is the target for this ferry craft (center), which is carrying liquid hydrogen tanks for use by lunar explorers. In the background in lower orbit is its operating base. Close to it is an external tank from a shuttle, which carries the liquid hydrogen tanks into Earth orbit. They are stored until needed in the dump complex shown on the left.

Left: Mining operations on the Moon next century. The material being mined here is an ore rich in oxygen. After mining, the ore is crushed and then processed to produce oxygen. Some of the oxygen is needed for pressurizing the living quarters of the mining base, while the rest is stored in liquid form for use as a rocket propellant.

Left: This wheel-like structure in far Earth orbit is a vast space colony housing 10,000 people. It measures about 1 mile (1.6 kilometers) in diameter. The inhabitants live in the outer 'tire' of the colony, which consists of a tube about 650 feet (200 meters) across. The structure rotates so as to create an artificial gravity. The outside of the colony is coated with rocky debris to shield the inmates from dangerous cosmic radiation.

Above: Inside the space colony an Earth-type landscape is created, and even farming activities can take place. The aim of the colony is to be self-supporting as far as possible. The materials required to construct the colony come not from Earth, but from the Moon or the asteroid belt.

Below: In the 22nd century space colonies will grow to enormous size. This view gives an idea of the scale of the operation. This cylindrical colony module measures some 20 miles (32 kilometers) long and 4 miles (7 kilometers) across and houses several hundred thousand people.